Jihadist Tendencies and Global Terrorism on Soft Targets

Jihadist Tendencies and Global Terrorism on Soft Targets

By

SARON MESSEMBE OBIA

Vij Books India Pvt Ltd
New Delhi (India)

Published by

Vij Books India Pvt Ltd
(Publishers, Distributors & Importers)
2/19, Ansari Road
Delhi – 110 002
Phones: 91-11-43596460, 91-11-47340674
Mob: 98110 94883
E-mail: contact@vipublishing.com
Web : www.vijbooks.in

ISBN: 978-93-90917-60-0 (Hardback)

ISBN: 978-93-90917-21-1 (Paperback)

ISBN: 978-93-90917-36-5 (ebook)

Dedicated to

To God almighty and Modika Efamba John

SECURITY IS HONOR-HUMILITY-TIMING

Contents

Acknowledgement

I would like to acknowledge Prof John M Nomikosis Director of the Research Institute for European and American Studies (RIEAS), Founding Editor, Journal of European and American Intelligence Studies, Noor Dahri, Excutive Director of the Islamic Theology of Counter Terrorism, Dr. Iryna Skrypchenko, Colonel (Rtr) Youssa Gedeon (PhD), and Sir Andrin Raj (PhD), Director of the International Association for Counter Terrorism and Security Professional South East Asia (IACSP SEA), for their invaluable guidance in the field of national and international security. As a researcher focusing on new security trends, such as; security of stadia and jihadist tendencies.

I would also like to express my sincere appreciation to Major (Rtr) Dieudonne Bilec, Commissaire Principale (Rtr) Siewe Levir, Tammy Waitt, Editorial Director of American Security Today, and Philomena O'Grady, Forensic Criminologist.

I am honored to have received positive and encouraging feedback from Mr. Fandjio Mougang B. (PhD) and, Mr. Modika M. Daniel whose critics and narratives on international security impacted me. I am also indebted to the legendary Rev. Ngalle Simon Njie, for both his professional advice and his personal kindness.

Introduction

The misinterpretation of words to describe a religion of peace and honor, demurs a strategic threat to the world. Islam is a way of life, inspired by the Holy Quran and Sunnah, and the teachings of prophet Mohammed. A Muslim is an individual who freely adheres to the Holy Scriptures but can be misled by radical teachings or religious order (fatwa) by an Imam with no conscience.

The 9/11 events established a social cleavage between Islam and Christianity, which is sometimes referred to a clash of cultures. Persons from diverse cultures adhere to extremist torts, misinterpretation of the holy Quran, and the quest to establish a self-proclaimed state under the banner of Islam. Religious belief is one of the aspect exploited by jihadists to legitimize their struggle, some of these actors and groups have been labelled terrorist organizations by the international community. From Al Qaeda in the Middle East to the African Maghreb, Boko Haram in Nigeria and Cameroon, Al Shabaab in East Africa and today, the Islamic State paints a new order.

Sun Tzu said, "You need not fear the results of a hundred battles." This work explores the quest for state creation, target selection and modus operandi of terrorist organizations from regional to international level. The Russian grand strategy is perceived as the best for countering violent extremism and jihadist tendencies on soft targets. The International Criminal Police (Interpol) and Federation Internationale de

Football Association (FIFA) security approaches are yet to be concretized. In essence, this work evaluates the tenacity and challenges facing the mutation of terrorist attacks and the menace on national security, geopolitical nature of states and the response of international organizations. It equally examines the dynamics of counter-terrorism and contemporary theories concerning jihadists' tendencies and terrorism.

Chapter One

International Security Trends

Introduction

Dialogue and religious tolerance are two core aspects necessary for lasting peace in the world. In Prince Hassan El Talal's book "Continuity, Innovation and Change", peacebuilding requires an attitude of sanctity and reverence for life, freedom, justice, poverty alleviation, and the environment's protection for personal and future generations. The world is facing a global security menace (jihadist tendencies and terrorism), necessitates adequate response.

The World Economic Forum of 2015 out pin an increase in terrorism activities during the last 15 years, reporting on a five-time increase in death rate in the year 2000. There has been a paradigm shift in target selection, as attacks on soft targets continue to increase (Paraskevas & Arendell: 2007). Terrorism differs in terms of places it occurs, actors engaged in the act and the implications following an attack (World Economic Forum: 2015). Before, sovereignty free actors (jihadists) attacked countries with intelligence loopholes; but civilians, mosque, schools are even attacked. However, policing methods are continuously developing with recovery strategies to curb these tendencies.

Civilization began in Africa, as such the continent is a pillar for other states, be in term of religion, education, politics and resources. Jihad, a religious crusade which emerge in the 19 century for education and religious revival in Nigeria and part of Cameroon, changed with the events of 9/11. State formation in pre-colonial Nigeria, a context of geographical proximity, biosocial relations and cultural contiguities were reviewed for proper development by Usman Dan fodio led jihad (1804-1817).

The 19th-century jihad restructured the Hausa (Habe) community with the creation of a new state, the Sokoto Caliphate. The nexus between pre-colonial state formation and social identity transformation along ethno-religious lincs are strategic aspect in modern religious fundamentalism. The transformation of social identities along ethno-religious lines appeals to the geopolitical nature of states. The Sokoto jihad had two significant implications.

Firstly, the reconfiguration of Hausa States led by Habe emirs into an empire and aborted the Habe dynasties, while enthroning the rule of the Fulani over states was strategic in Hausa land. Secondly, the cosmopolitanism ideology of the

Hausa initiated a new ethno-religious identity, the Hausa-Fulani. These implications were significantly influential in the trajectories of social identity formation in the Caliphate.

The arrival of Muslim Fulani clerics in Hausa land, their revolutionary teachings and the Usman Dan Fodio led Jihad in the 19th century halted the course of development of the Hausa States. It ended the Hausa dynasties and transformed pcople ethno religious stance, such that, they perceived post-colonial Nigeria as Hausa-Fulani territory. These conditions necessitating the evolution of the Hausa state formations before the interception by the Fulani jihadists, and the ethno-religious transformation of part of northern Nigeria into the Sokoto Caliphate.

Bako (1999) argues that, the development led to an ideological base on teachings against the state order in that era before the execution of Jihad. Suffice to note that, the call for Jihad took the pattern of contemporary civil society. According to Sulaiman, Dan Fodio's jihad moulded men and women to adhere to his ideas and share his aspirations to bring an umma dedicated to Islam in order to transform society. He trained persons and created his own community of scholars, teachers and saints. It was through these persons (Talaba) that he spread his message; and as well, formed the inner core of the movement.

The Jama'a (community) was formed in Degel, the Gobir state and was transformed into a militant group in the subsequent years to execute the jihad (Bako, 1999: 7989). The people who joined the Jama'a were motivated by varied objectives. Bello's classification of the community presented these motives into ten categories depending on their involvement. Sulaiman (n/d) cited Bello thus:

The first nine include those who had joined the Jama'a for purely political reasons because it offered a refuge for the oppressed; those who, being Fulani, had joined it on tribal considerations and had cause to 'despise the non Fulani, even if they were educated, pious or mujahidin'; those whose reason for their membership was no more than 'fashion'; scholars whose fortunes had been drained by the revolutionary momentum unleashed by the Jama'a, and who had no alternative but to join in order to survive; and those who were in the Jama'a because it offered material benefits.

There were still others who rode the prestigious crest of Jama'a, even though they had been attracted by the world and the devil,' and had abandoned its goals. Those born within the Jama'a and remained in it, not by absolute conviction, but by birth, who were not keen to learn the values and objectives that the movement stood for. Other were swept by currents into the body of the Jama'a: they did not know why they were there, nor did they belong there, either by orientation or conviction; hence, depression became their lot. The genuine members of the Jama'a, who comprised one out of the ten categories, were those 'guided not by the world but by Allah, giving up property, power and family for life to come'.

Notwithstanding these circumstances, which motivated the people, the objective of Usman Dan Fodio was to mobilize people towards embracing and joining the Jama'a to fulfil the task of jihad, rethinking Pre-Colonial State Formation and Ethno-Religious Identity Transformation in Hausa land under the Sokoto Caliphate.

An understanding of the concept of jihad is vital for ideological legitimization of political Islam in contemporary society. The concept has a complex and contested historical precedent drawn from the Quran and the Hadith, which controversial in relation to contemporary sociopolitical circumstances (Euben 2002: p. 21). This makes the true meaning of the term ambiguous. Nonetheless, there is a tendency to reify jihad, making it synonymous with armed struggle ("holy war") (see Knudsen 2002a: p. 12).

Thus, the term is now often used as a conventional shorthand not only for the Islamic revival in the Middle East (considered a "jihadist backlash") but also for the menace pose to Western democracy, in Islamists quest for world hegemony "global jihad". While the notion of a "global jihad" is easily discounted, a more difficult question is whether the Islamist movement is premised on an armed struggle against opponents and enemies.

Genesis of Global Terrorism

The 1980 Iranian embassy siege did not only expose Margaret Thatcher's administrative strategy to response to security menace, but the world to future trends. At the end of the 18th century, the French revolution was described by the Dictionnaire de l'Académie française as a regime of terror (Hoffman: 1998). Ironically, the term had a positive connotation in the yesteryears to implement order, structure, and reestablish the hierarchy in the divided society that had followed the French revolution (1789 until 1799).

Moreover, the term held together with the notions of virtue, trust and justice, as described by Robespierre in one of his speeches: Terror is nothing but justice, prompt, severe and inflexible; it is, therefore, an emanation of virtue. After Robespierre‹s execution by guillotine, the interpretation of the term changed due to abuse of power, illicit implications by some leaders (Bienvenu: 1970). Fascist era, is a good example to explain how terrorism was used as a system for mass repression, against citizens in order to justify cruel acts (Hoffman: 1998).

Terrorism is the use of political and religious authority or power for geostrategic, geo-economics reason to justify a situational conflict of ideas within and out of states. The first to provide a distinction between terrorism and aspiration for independence from colonial powers was Yasir Arafat, the chairman of the Palestine Liberation Organization (PLO), during a speech to the United Nations General Assembly in November 1974. The difference between the revolutionary and terrorist `lies in the reason for which each fights. For whoever stands by a just cause and fights for the freedom and liberation of his land from the invaders, the settlers and the colonialists, cannot possibly be called terrorist (Hoffman 1998).

In 1960s and 1970s, Quebecois separatist groups Front de Liberation du Quebec (FLQ) and the Euskadi ta Askatasuna, or Freedom for the Basque Homeland (Basque ETA), adopted terrorism as a radical, ideologically crusade. Hofmann (1998) argues that, these groups were seeking international coverage, along with sympathy and support. The term grab international recognition following series of suicide bombings directed against American institutions and military in the Middle East, a region noted for state-sponsored terrorism (Iran, Iraq, Libya and Syria) (Hoffmann:1998). Conflicts across the world are no longer associated with traditional notions of war, as fighting between armed forces of two or more engage in such acts.

The US Federal Bureau of Investigation (FBI) has three core aspects in defining terrorism: Involve violent acts or deviant behaviour violate federal or state norm and is a menace to human security; to intimidate or coerce a civilian population; to influence the policy of a government by intimidation or coercion; or to affect government operation through mass casualty, assassination, or abduction; usually coordinated either from a foreign territory or within in which their perpetrators operate or seek asylum (FBI: 2018).

The FBI recognizes politics as a major agenda of terrorism (to influence the policy of a government). Critical enough to understand Ronald Reagan's distinction between terrorist and freedom fighters (which underlines the idea mentioned by Yasir Arafat). Effective antiterrorist action has also been thwarted by the claim that, as the quip goes, "One man's terrorist is another man's freedom fighter." (Reagan: 1986). Freedom fighters need not terrorize a population to adhere to an ideology. Freedom fighters target the military forces in order to oust dictators, struggle to liberate citizens from oppression and to establish a system of governance which reflects the will of the people (Reagan: 1986).

Clash of Cultures within Islam

Understanding cultural dynamics will require us to retrace the political legacy of the Prophet Muhammad. When the Prophet died in the early 7th Century, he left the religion of Islam and an 'Islamic State' in the Arabian Peninsula with around one hundred thousand Muslims. The rhetoric over a successor of Prophet led to the birth of a new Islamic state which creates divide. A group of Muslims (the larger group) elected Abu Bakr, a close companion of the Prophet as the next caliph (leader) of the Muslims and their leaders.

However, the minority believed that the Prophet's son in-law, Ali, should be made caliph. Muslims who believed that Abu Bakr, should be the next leader were Sunni, while those who believed in Ali were Shia. The two cultures (Shia and Sunni) agree that Muhammad was the lone prophet. Sunni Muslims pray five times a day, whereas Shia Muslims can combine prayers to pray three times a day. The practice of Muttah marriage, a temporary marriage, is also permitted in Shia Islam, but Sunnis considered it forbidden. Islamic State's agenda has been linked to Sunni tribal groups, members of Saddam Hussein's army and intelligence services.

The Sunni believes that the first four caliphs–Mohammed's successors–rightfully took his place as emirs. They recognize the heirs of the four caliphs as legitimate religious emirs. Their leadership marked the Arab world until the break-up of the Ottoman Empire following the end of the First World War. Contrary to Shiites, the narrative was that only the heir of the fourth caliph Ali was the legitimate successor of Mohammed. Scott Appleby, a professor of history at the University of Notre Dame, "Shiite Muslims, who are concentrated in Iran, Iraq, and Lebanon, [believe they] had suffered the loss of divinely guided political leadership" at the time of the Imam's disappearance. Not until the ascendancy of Ayatollah Ruhollah Khomeini in 1978 did they believe that they had once again begun to live under the authority of a legitimate religious figure.

In a special 9-11 edition of the Journal of American History, Appleby argued that, the Shiite outlook is far different from the Sunni's, a highly significant difference: for Sunni Muslims, approximately 90 percent of the Muslim world, the loss of the caliphate after World War I was a historical challenge to the caliph, the guardian of Islamic law and the Islamic state. Sunni pundits (jihadists) emerged from nations such as Egypt and India, where the Western system provided a new model leading to the abolition of the Islamic caliphate.

Abolition of Islamic Caliphate

In 1928, four years after the abolishment of concept of religious caliphate, an Egyptian school teacher Hasan al-Banna founded the first Islamic fundamentalist movement in the Sunni world, the Muslim Brotherhood (al-Ikhwan al-Muslimun). The European culture is always perceived to be a breach of Islamic tradition; dressing code (half-naked women), liquors, satiric newspapers, and other vices. As the Islamic world subscribed to European "schools and scientific and cultural institutes casting doubt and heresy into the souls of its sons and taught them how to demean themselves from religion and cultural heritage to the Western system."

Most distressing to al-Banna and his followers was what they saw as the rapid moral decline of the religious establishment, including the leading sheikhs, or religious scholars, at Al-Azhar, the grand mosque and centre of Islamic learning in Cairo. The clerical leaders had become compromised and corrupted by their alliance with the indigenous ruling elites who had succeeded the European colonial masters.

Osama bin Laden, a Sunni Muslim, perceived the end of the reign of the caliphs in the 1920s as catastrophic, in a videotape made after 9-11. The tape, broadcast by Al Jazeera on October 7, 2001, he proclaimed: "What America is tasting now is only a copy of what we have tasted. ... Our Islamic nation has been tasting the same for more [than] eighty years, of humiliation and disgrace, its sons killed and their blood spilled, its sanctities desecrated."

The Syrian Civil War and the birth of ISIS

Professor Hans Kung posed; 'No peace among nations without peace among the religions and no peace among the religions without dialogue between the religions'. He added, 'No peace without justice and no justice without forgiveness and compassion'. Dialogue and agreement must be conscientiously applied and maintained to create love, care, trust, and confidence bonds. Its prerequisite is proper education and learning from one another.

Terrorist groups which are currently threatening the world peace and stability are; Islamic State, Hamas, Hezbollah, Boko Haram, Taliban, Al Qaeda as well as others. A terrorist group emerged from the Middle East named IS parading as freedom fighters. They were later responsible for a number of attacks in Europe, including the two most significant ones analyzed: Paris 2015 and Brussels 2016. An overview of the IS developments and consequently on the attacks which followed within Europe.

There is also reason to caution against research on "Islamic terrorism" that reiterates dogmatic accounts of Islam and Sharia's inherent tendency towards extreme violence. This narrative is linked to contemporary in the tendency to give precedence to the most violent movements (Bangstad 2002: p. 6) and the views of their leaders (Appleby 1997, JPS 2002) rather than those of their members and supporters.

There is as yet little serious research on violence perpetrated in the name of religion (see Juergensmeyer 2000) compared to the many simplistic accounts touting the threat of a "holy war" based on a biased reading of Islam's founding texts.

The Islamic State is reputable for violence. It asserts control, but its ruthless tactics synonymous with guerrilla warfare aspiring to establish a caliphate is a dooms day history in the modern system. It is considered to be a clandestine organization. Despite her cyber crusade and analysis generated since 2011, verifiable facts concerning its leadership and structure remain challenging. The picture is obscured by the misleading propaganda of the State itself and by the questionable accounts of people who claim to be familiar with it. It is a movement that changes global security dynamics, from terrorism through insurgency towards proto-statehood (Richard Barrett, 2014).

The jihadist group (ISIS) made its debut on the political and international scene in 2014. After the military conquest in Syria and Iraq, a reconfiguration was made to a caliphate which appealed for supremacy of Ibrahim Awad Ibrahim alBadri al-Samarrai (Abu Bakr al-Baghdadi) (BBC: 2015).

In 2014, IS control argued that it covered 210,000km2 back in 2014, but still lost territories that very year to Iraq and Syria. The crusaders (jihadists) argued the fact that they wanted to restore the order of God on Earth and that they were defending the Muslim community against the disbelievers and against Islamic culture. The US invasion in Iraq in 2004 re-organized the group, as she now held different names, among which the best known are IS (Islamic State) and "Islamic State in Iraq and the Levant" (ISIS) (BBC: 2015).

Statistics reveal the spread of IS in Middle East has an impact on Europe as in 2014, 200,000 engaged on a sea journey to seek asylum in Europe compared to 60,000 the previous year, according to statistics from the U.N. refugee agency UNHCR. Security trends keep changing as fighters join refugee camps or use refugee status to seek asylum to enter the Western world to perpetrate attacks. EUROPOL's statistics suggest that between 3922 and 4294 citizens are foreign fighters from the E.U. Out of which 30 percent returned and 14 percent were confirmed dead (ICCT, 2016). IS now recruits fighters, who can use their E.U. passports to travel across the continent undetected because of the open borders policy, then enter Turkey and finally move across Syria.

Abu Bakr and followers regarded the Syrian uprising as a distraction from its Iraq-centric crusade, forbidding even their Syrian members from joining the rebellion. The uprising spread and became more violent with the arrival of nine Syrian members headed by Abu Mohammed al Golani in Northern Syria in mid-2011. The protein alliance between Golani and Zawahiri brought in al Qaeda operatives from Pakistan and to work with him to stage attacks. The trends of Golani pose a problem to the leadership of Abu Bakr in April 2013, Golani refused to acknowledge Jabhat al Nusra li Ahl al-Sham (the Support Front for the People of the Levant) was a branch of The Islamic State of Iraq, and appealed to Zawahiri to rule on the matter, so making public his own association with al Qaeda.

On 29 June 2014, following rapid territorial gains, which included the capture of Mosul on 10 June, ISIS declared the revival of the Caliphate, naming it The Islamic State and Abu Bakr as Caliph Ibrahim. The declaration was intended as a rallying call to all observant Muslims, but in particular, those who shared the Salafist/takfiri views expressed by The Islamic State, and so draw away support from like-minded groups in Syria, including al Nusra, that might compete for recruits and resources.

The declaration was also a direct challenge to the authority of Zawahiri and the role of Mullah Omar, who until then had been the undisputed Amir al Mu'minin (Leader of the Faithful). At Friday prayers at the Grand Mosque of al Nuri in Mosul on 4 July, in his first address as Caliph, Abu Bakr claimed that he had reluctantly accepted the title at the behest of the community of Islamic scholars, albeit that they remained unidentified and silent.

The rapid conquest of Mosul and declaration of a Caliphate caused a brief surge in new recruits, but did not achieve the impact which supporters of The Islamic State had expected or hoped for. Indeed, there is evidence to suggest that the reaction among extremists to the declaration of the Caliphate overall was initially negative, though following the start of coalition airstrikes on August 23 2014, support picked up.

Although the consensus opinion was that the declaration of a Caliphate would be premature because the group's control of territory was not yet firm enough, Abu Bakr decided that he had more to gain than to lose and may also have been deceived by his own appreciation of his historical role. Jabhat al Nusra has since shown that it faces similar disagreements over raising its status, in this case, to become an Islamic Emirate or State. A supposedly leaked tape of Golani announcing an Islamic State in four areas of Syria under al Nusra control on 12 July 2014 was followed by a partial retraction and some confusion.

In 2014, Belgium became the first E.U. country to experience an attack by a foreign fighter returning from Syria when a man of French national– Mehdi Nemmouche opened fire in a Jewish museum in Brussels, killing four people.

The following year coordinated attacks were perpetrated in Paris, 130 killed and injured around 352 others, according to the NATO Review Magazine (NATO: 2015). Based on the investigations, eight of the plotters were foreign fighters returning from Syria. The men identified as carrying out the attacks were French nationals. The leader was a well-known Belgian foreign fighter, Abdelhamid Abaaoud (Brisard: 2015).

In January 2016, police killed two young Belgian men who had travelled to Syria. One of the suspects appeared in an IS video in driving a car in the desert with casualties. The federal prosecutor, Eric Van Der Sypt, said a terrorist attack may only have been hours away: This operation stopped a major terrorist attack from taking place. One saw a second potential Paris attack been averted (The Guardian: 2015). The EU has three narratives for combating radicalization and recruitment to terrorism: disruption of activities of networks and individuals who draw people into terrorism; ensure that voices of mainstream opinion prevail over those of extremism; and promote yet more vigorously security, justice, democracy and opportunity for all. (EU: 2005).

Chapter Two

Crime Theories and Extremism

Introduction

The inter-relation of ideologies in political science and political philosophy (Cohen, 2008, p. 1; Freeden, 1996, p. 132; Knight, 2006; Vincent, 2004, p. 73.) is undisputed to global security challenges. Ideologies tend to push argument in an ad hominem direction, which is perhaps why academic writers tend to write about their practices and theories, as if they can be considered separately from ideologies. The consequence of this until now has been that the study of ideologies has become what it should not have become: a coterie activity. Hassan Abu Hanieh exposed several aspects that appeal to radicalizations and prerequisite for ISIS sympathizers. These are but not limited to; failure of the nation-state, the symbolism of the Islamic Caliphate, the emergence of sectarianism, Western Imperialism and information and communication technology.

Are Knudsen (2003), an examination of political Islam, classifies sociological theories under three aspects; civilization, social and textual. The concept of civilization throwbacks to the sociopolitical configuration of Arab states from the 18- 19th century (dynastic theories) and the emergence of alliances in the 20th century, reconfiguring some states as super power. The second aspect focuses on

Islamic revival, linked to sociopolitical trends (cultural duality theories and state culture theories). At the same time, the textual consecration focuses on Islamic crusade based Holy Scriptures and doctrine as well as religious worship.

A. CONTEMPORARY THEORIES

1. The New Cyberterrorism Theory

Validation of a theory is based on its strategy or grand strategy in relation to the field of study or issues to address (Kennedy, 1991). Each nation usually has an explicit or implicit strategy on how to respond to global security trends, as most typically have a forum where experts get together like the National Security Council for the United States. Grand strategy is usually the domain of scholars (Waltz 1979; Gaddis 1982; Heymann 2003; Ikenberry 2002; Mead 2004; Nye 2002), as well as anyone else, who writes on related subjects like global terrorism, jihadist tendencies and cyber criminality (Clark 2003; Frum & Perle 2003; Kagan 2003; Brzezinski 2004; Cronin & Ludes 2004; Etzioni 2004; Ferguson 2004; Hart 2004; Stevenson 2004; Barnett 2005).

Before September 11, 2001, George W. Bush, presidential candidate, had warned "American forces are overused and underfunded precisely when they are confronted by a host of new threats and challenges the spread of weapons of mass destruction, the rise of cyberterrorism and the proliferation of missile technology." Bush narrative appeal for criminal tactics of the 1960s with the hijacked commercial airliners by Palestinian terror groups, Popular Front for the Liberation of Palestine (PFLP) and the Abu Nidal Organization in pursuit of their political and ideological objectives (Sources: Haaretz, The Palestine Liberation Organization, p. 137, Britannica, RAND, BBC News). This led to the creation of the Office of

Cyberspace Security in the White House by President Bush is strategic.

In a representative observation in April 2003, Tom Ridge (director of the Department of Homeland Security) reintegrated that "Terrorists can sit at one computer connected to one network and can create worldwide havoc". "They don't necessarily need a bomb or explosives to cripple a sector of the economy or shut down a power grid." These warnings which correlate with a survey of 725 cities conducted in 2003 by the National League of Cities, which ranked cyberterrorism alongside biological and chemical weapons at the top of a list of city officials' fears. Critical enough to recapture the first-ever terrorist hijacking perpetrated in 1968 by Popular Front for the Liberation of Palestine (PFLP), targeting an Israeli El Al airliner from Rome to Tel Aviv and diverted it to Algeria, abducted 12 persons and released them in exchange for 16 Arab prisoners (Sources: Council on Foreign Relations, BBC News, New York Times, International Encyclopedia of Terrorism, p. 233, RAND).

The new cyber terrorism theory examines challenges within three narratives; doctrine, command and time. The interest in cyber-terrorism by some religious extremists (jihadists) in the quest of 'Muslim Supremacy or Dominance' through global 'Jihad' demurs a formidable fop. Attacks coordinated by radical religious clerics like Abubakar Shekau of Boko-Haram, American-born radical imam Anwar alAwlaki and Imam Samudra of 2002 Bali bombing which caused several casualties are centered on radical fatwa.

Command and time remain two strategic factors of cyberterrorism. For jihadists, tendencies are not only limited to science, resources, courage and speed (timing). Dorothy E. Denning's presentation on 'The Jihadi Cyberterror Threat' expose most individuals who engage in cyber-terrorism have gone through formal education in Information Communication Technology (computer science, computer engineering, and information science) and security studies. Their knowledge and expertise (radicals, terrorists or militia) pose a global menace. As new fractions of the terrorist organization continue to emerge with different patterns in attacks, drones pose a strategic menace, with international actors like Islamic State seeking media coverage to boost aspirants through their strategies. For example, in 2016, Brussels' Zaventem airport was attacked by three ISIS suicide bombers. The same year three ISIS suicide bombers killed 45 people and wounded more than 230 at Istanbul's Ataturk Airport. (Sources: Reuters, Heavy, Agence France-Presse, Telegraph, New York Times, Heavy, NBC, CNN)

New Cyber Terrorism Theory

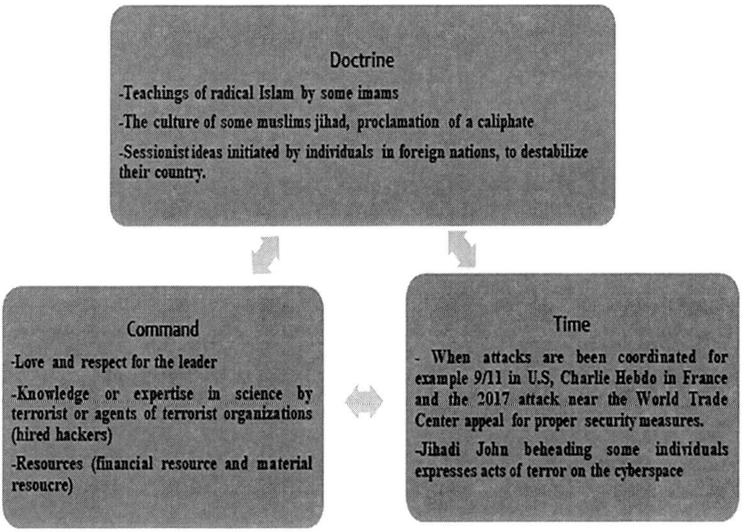

The new cyber terrorism theory analyzes global security challenges. Doctrine is one of the fundamental path to radicalization and global terrorism, which is usually eminent from the term 'jihad'. The word is used by some religious clerics to bring their followers to perpetrate violence on targeted states and communities. According to Asma Barlas, jihad is mentioned 36 times in the holy Quran, referring to a moral duty, in different narratives such as jihad of the soul (life), the tongue (propaganda), or the pen (article, presentations and strategies). One of the core principles of Islam is: "Good and bad are not equal. Replace evil by good" (Holy Qur'an 41:34), but extremists exploit these flaws to draw followers or sympathizers to perpetrate jihadists tendencies.

Jihadists tendencies are often perpetrated following religious commands issued by spiritual leaders, which some are usually radical religious clerics with the crusade of global jihad and need to establish an Islamic Caliphate. Fatwa refers to a religious command issued by religious cleric in the Islamic world. The concept of Fatwa is heavily disputed in the Muslim world. Fatwa is an Islamic term for a legal opinion given by a Mufti or cleric in a situation in which Islamic norm is not clear or interpreted differently (Mah-Rukh Ali, 2015).

- In 1979 fatwa by Iranian leader Ayatollah Khomeini relating to the death sentence of Salman Rushdie for his book 'Satanic Verses'. The question has always been who can issue a fatwa? Religious clerics or charismatic leaders can issue a Fatwa, with no requirement or formal education. Unlike an Alim (scholar) who requires formal education, must study Islamic Fiqh and jurisprudence extensively.

- Saudi Wahabi cleric Sheikh Mohamad al-Arefe, was the first to issue a fatwa appealing for Sunni women to present themselves for sexual Jihad in Syria. Their logic is that Islam is like Christianity, a missionary religion in which God's message is primordial; anything forbidden becomes "halal" in times of Jihad, according to extremists.

There exist several types of jihad; but the focus is on the radical crusade of ISIS and some other jihadists groups in Africa. For example; the 'Nikkah ul Jihad' is a religious duty inspired by controversial Fatwa, such as ordering women to offer themselves as sexual servants to Jihadists. Men are granted permission to marry a woman for a week or hours, to have "halal" sex with her in order to pursue their Jihadi mission. A survey conducted in Tunisia revealed that, most women rescued from jihadist capture zones were pregnant, some infected with certain diseases as they were expected to have sex with 10-20 men.

Timing is a strategic factor in the analysis of crime scenes and attacks. Terrorism and violent extremism has led to the development of a new course in the field of security; strategic response to terrorism, terrorism spots, counterterrorism of stadia and armed security threats. This paper will be exploring timing in relation to terrorists' attacks on stadia, following certain parameters below; Safety and security in and around sports venues.

Mega Sporting events are increasingly targeted by terrorist organizations or jihadists groups. Terrorists usually launch their attack to attract for global recognition because of the global convergence and recognition of sports. Safety and security of lives and properties are important aspects of any sports organization and management. For instance, people are now conscious of where they go and what they do following the Stade de Paris attack in 2015. Some sports persons will want to know the security arrangements and assurance of sporting venues before they attend events. There is a likelihood of people not attending sports for on field viewership or spectatorship, especially when there is a security threat. Some spectators prefer to watch the game at home with safety and security assurance than going to the stadium to risk their lives and properties.

The relevance of this theory as it concerns international security is to caution intelligence agencies and security experts about the threats posed by migration and globalization, particularly the imminent threat of drones. In criminology and criminal justice, the theory predicts as best the unpredictable as well as explains or understands thoughts in the mind of jihadists which are hard to conceptualize. It also advocates for proper surveillance and background check of foreign students engage in the field of IT and Security Studies in vulnerable countries to restrain future security threats. For example, Mohammed Emwazi (Jihadi John) IT graduate in England, who claimed the security services were ruining his life and Sami Omar Al-Hussayen Saudi CS graduate student at university of Idaho studying computer security, charged for operating websites used to recruit terrorists, raise funds, and disseminate inflammatory rhetoric (Dorothy E. Denning, The Jihadi Cyberterror Threat).

2. The General Theory of Islam

The general theory of Islam defines with consideration the implication of Islamic Shariah (law) in daily life (see, OSCE Confreence in Baku, Azerbaijin, 10-11 October 2002, P. 38). According to Islamic teachings, the prophet provided laws governing the natural universe but also rules for human conduct in all aspects of life. Critical to say unlike natural order, which follows its predetermined laws, mankind has the freedom to rebel and follow its own "man-made" laws, which is, however, a form of unbelief (shirk) (source: The Role of Religion and Belief in The Fight Against Terrorism, OSCE Conference in Baku, Azerbaijan, 10-11 October 2002). Non-submission to the will of Allah is not only an act of ingratitude (kufr) for divine mercies but also a choice for evil and misery in this world and punishment in the life hereafter.

The rhetoric over religious fundamentalism is based on its chapter, Islamic way of life, which highlights; Islamic State, jihad, shariah law and fatwa, most at times misinterpreted to orchestra conflicts focusing on culture, resource capture and political configuration of states. According to Imam Dr Abduljalil Sajid, most people misinterpret the term Islam and Muslims. Islam should be used exclusively for the way of life based upon divine sources: The Quran, the word of God, while Muslims as human beings are free to abide by, or deviate from, divine guidance based on conscience.

Jihadist tendencies are usually linked to prominent medieval theologians and legal scholar like Ibn Taymiyya and the 20th century Egyptian intellectual and Islamic activist Sayyid Qutb. They were the godfather of modern revolutionary Islam. They promulgated the three core elements of Islamic way of life (unity); din (religion), dunya (community) and dawla (state). The clue of Islamic Shariah in the Quran is that "those who forget God eventually forget themselves" (59:19), and their individual and corporate personalities disintegrate.

Asma Barlas's argue that, the holy war is different between Muslims and non-Muslims. From his reading of the Qur'an, jihad means a "striving" or "struggle," and not war – much less a holy war. The question is what makes a war holy? He observed the Qur'an does not use "jihad" for war and forbids coercion in religion, such a war is not an Islamic tool. As such, jihad is considered unjust because of its religious inclination to some researchers like John Laffin in alarmist Holy War: Islam Fights to the Hindu revivalist, Suhas Majumdar's Jihād: The Islamic Doctrine of Permanent War.

In an interview conducted with some Moroccans, they argue that the situation in the Arab world is a program developed 30 years ago to destroy Islam through internal conflicts. They equally exposed that social media is one of the predominant tools used to incriminate and devilise Islam to promote the arms industry to support other cause movements.

Islam is a religion of peace with different cultures just like Christianity. Verkaik's (2016) raised two pertinent questions after Emwazi death in November 2015 following a U.S. air strike; what led Emwazi to come to him for help in the first place? And why do hundreds of Britons want to join Islamic State? Verkaik made an interesting observation about those who inflict terrorism; agencies involved in the protection citizens sometimes employ tactics that have unintended results (human rights violation and religious coertion). For example, Emwazi's story about being grilled at London's Heathrow Airport, was already a path to radicalization, when his Qur'an was allegedly placed on the floor by one of his interrogators. He was from a Kuwaiti family that migrated to London. Like Jihadi John, others integrate the society through education, avoiding suspicion. He resurfaced after been baptized as Jihadi John, stunned the world with series of cruel executions which the Qur'an prohibits. One of the principles of Islam is that: "Good and bad are not equal. Replace evil by good" (Holy Qur'an 41:34).

3. Saron Messembe Conflict Theory

Bad governance in some states are the cause of internal wrangling and coups, poor managements of resources and totalitarian regimes. There are two types of conflicts; positive conflicts (constructive conflict) and Negative conflict (destructive conflict, violent extremism and jihadists' tendencies), which are elements of geosciences (geopolitics and geostrategy). Though perceived as an essential tool of human security, it explores issues related to the clash of cultures or civilization, particularly religious fanatism. The theory's principal idea is that the security approach to some social vices is critical to religious extremists.

The Westphalia treaty of 1648 demurs a major aspect in contemporary issues (global war on terror, extremism and jihadist tendencies), resource capture, cultural deviance (Christian and Muslim rift) and geostrategic trends (acquisition of new and former territories before independence) and moderate politics. Conflicts are as a result of illegal intervention in foreign states, human rights violation, cultural deviance (non-respect of identity and religious leaders), breach international norms and protocols, and the rise of sovereignty free actors (terrorist) with diverse stances about contemporary issues (doctrine of sharia law by some Muslim radicals).

The theory provides the best approach to combat radicalization and violent extremists. Once a group or association is identified and classified, either as legal or illegal, the government should negotiate in case of any hostage taken (conflict management), initiate disarmament, demobilization and reintegration of formal actors engaged in deviance behaviours against the state for peace and stability (if weapons are dropped).

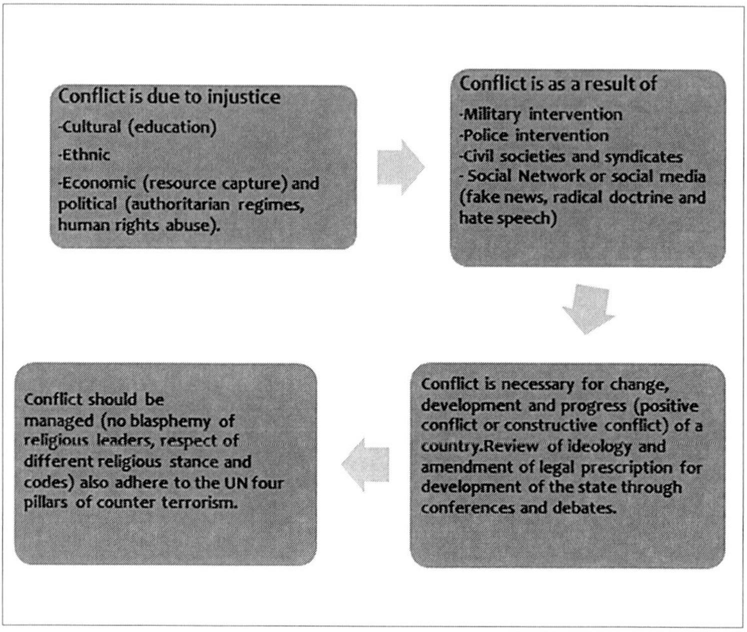

The relevance of the theory as concerns human security is to caution states and regional communities on the result during security intervention in relation to cultural conflict (education), economic conflict (resource capture example quest for oil, gold and wood just to name a few) and political conflict (authoritarian regimes and nepotism). The theory also highlights how violation of self-defense rule and human rights abuse (abduction, rape and arbitrary arrest) and the involvement of some multinational companies (internet blackout) in politics contribute to emerging threats. It advocates for censorship on social media networking sites and request government machinery to engage against Islamophobia and discrimination at all levels.

B. SOCIOLOGICAL THEORIES

In the Arab world, the spiritual leader is superior to the political leader. Are Knudsen pose that, the increasing jihadist tendencies in the Middle East, but is neither illogical nor irrational. Islamist groups in the region are usually transformed into peaceful political parties successfully contesting municipal and national elections, but there exist a "gloom and doom" approach that portrays Islamism as an illegitimate political expression and a potential menace to the West ("Old Islamism"), and a nuanced understanding of the current democratization of the Islamist movement that is now taking place throughout the Middle East ("New Islamism").

This importance of understanding the ideological roots of the "New Islamism" is foregrounded along with the need for thorough first-hand knowledge of Islamist movements and their adherents. As social movements, lay emphasis on the social cleavage in society, with the need to understanding and harness the aspirations of the poorer sections of society but also of the middle class. A general problem with the term political Islam is that it tends to imply "an illegitimate extension of the Islamic tradition outside of the properly religious domain it has historically occupied" (Hirschkind 1997: p. 12) "prefixing" Islam to create a bewildering conceptual plurality, which, to name but a few, includes; radical Islam, militant Islam, extremist Islam, revolutionary Islam and fundamentalist Islam.

1. Dynastic Theory

The first sociological theory was developed by the medieval historian Ibn Khaldun (1333–1406) in his masterpiece, Muqaddimah (1377 (1967)) on the notion of the Islamic state and explaining the social cleavage between political (royalty) and religious (caliphate). Khaldun's book developed a sociological and historiographic account of the cyclical rise and fall of urban civilizations. The theory focuses on "group solidarity" (asabiyya) is a major factor for new dynastic ruins, particularly in the Arab world, with statesmen alliance to other regional poles. These inter-regional poles have certain populace actors as well as made others to be removed. Importantly, Khaldun pose that the only way for the creation of an Islamic state was an issue of asabiyya, that is social solidarity, but on the religious authority of a fatwa and Sharia. Khaldun's narrative exposed the misguided concept of some thinkers by elaborating on "the differentiation between religious and secular leadership" (Moaddel 2002b: p. 367).

2. Cultural Duality Theory

The cultural duality theory is a strategic response to the challenges of crisis theories, which expose the tension between the power of the state and the religious leadership (Moaddel 2002b: p. 372). When authority of an emir or imam is restrained and certain privileges removed, it orchestrates political opposition critical for the formation of alliances and creation of militia groups. The theory adapts to the cultural norm of Shia Islam, where religious leaders have autonomous positions than in Sunni Islam. The cultural duality model is a conceptual framework in understanding the rise of revolutionary movements in Iran (1977–79). Actors like Shii ulama (clergy) exposed their charisma and authority by challenging the state. The theory is usually criticized because it limits the propaganda of the jihadist crusade but expresses the tension between religion and regime.

3. State Culture Theory

State culture theory examines one of the fundamental hold up of extremism nowadays. First, Islamic revival is an outcome of the tension between regime and religion, but points out a dynamic approach in policing terrorism and jihadist tendencies. A breach in religious principles will limit the status quo and even cause an Islamist backlash. For example, the rise of radical Islamism in Algeria in the early 1970s was based on land reform and leftist policies with a nepotistic inclination (see Political Violence). Another example is the radicalization of the Egyptian Muslim Brothers in response to increasing authoritarian regime after a military coup in 1952. The assassination of the MB founder Hassan al-Banna, and torture of its followers served increased the level of radicalization by the chief ideologue, Sayyid Qutb, leading to a change in policy and tactics (Kepel 1985). The major idea of the state culture theory is cultural conflict between Islam and secularism, the path to extremism and jihadist tendencies describe Esposito as "militant secular fundamentalism", Islamic crusade. Examples of this phenomenon may be found in Libya, Egypt, Syria and Iran.

CHAPTER THREE

TRANSNATIONAL ORGANIZATION AND SOCIAL DEVIANCE

Introduction

The globalization era changed the dynamics of international relation theories and the development of transnational networks (Al Qaeda, ISIS, Boko Haram, the freemasonry and the anti-globalization the Illuminati). ISIS has proven to be a global menace from its modus operandi, target selection and operations coordinated out of Syria. Though the organization's central command is in Syria, during operations, tactical freedom is given to local leaders to adapt their actions.

IS capability to strike at will and at almost any chosen target is critical to nation-states, particularly to North and West Africa. Target selection is based on group capability, population and resources for the execution plan. Soft targets continue to be of preference for mass casualties. This preference for soft targets is strategic to critical infrastructure such as power grids, stadiums and transportation hubs. Cyber-attacks follow the same trend with the proliferation of drones, a major weapon for counter-terrorism, a future threat if used by jihadists.

The escalation of violence and massive attacks represents a new dawn in IS strategy in Europe. The intended randomness in target selection urges Member States to 'expect the unexpected'. Unexpected events, however, are not by definition incidents that have never happened but the emergence of modern trends. For example, an attack by drones by ISIS will appeal to the countervailing shift in counter-terrorism strategy in the world. The weapon of choice is the AK 47, which is usually brandished by ISIS on various logos and its affiliates. The AK 47 is easily purchased and usually acquired in the country where an attack is planned or in a neighboring state from where it is easily transported.

The tactics employed by the Islamic State are considered to be guerrilla warfare. Most of its core leadership are ex Ba'athists, and have been involved in violent opposition to the Iraqi state since 2003. Several were held at various times in US detention camps, and some escaped from Iraqi prisons during the 'Breaking the Walls' campaign of the predecessor group, the Islamic State of Iraq, from July 2012 to July 2013. Her knowledge and experience have changed the pattern of policing terrorism and jihadists' tendencies. Also, she attempted to consolidate its territorial gains by developing an administrative organ that attracts fighters and brings in civilian technocrats (hackers, programmers and network security engineers) for operations like the 9/11.

In combination with the 2015 bombing of a Russian airliner in Egypt by ISIS, attacks in Suruç and Ankara (Turkey), Beirut and Baghdad, the Paris attacks exposed a broader strategy of the organization's aspirations to 'monopolize' member states of the European Union. Despite Europol's meeting of 30 November and 1 December 2015, with members of the First Response Network (FRN) of the European Union on the threat of all religiously inspired terrorism and to evaluate the risk of being targeted by ISIS, security challenges are still obvious. Al-Qaeda continues to threaten western countries and may even be triggered to put words into action by competing with ISIS, an organization that is now attacking targets that were previously considered to be out of their reach.

Terrorist Attacks and State Deviance on Citizens

A. EXPLORING ATTACKS ON SOFT TARGETS

1. Violent attack on Sri Lanka's cricket team in the Pakistani in 2009

Sport is one of the major tool used by statesmen to solve political and socioeconomic issues around the world. The link between sport and terrorism is the role of engagement of paramilitary forces when opposed to social deviance within the milieu. For example, Palestinian Black September group attack on Israeli athletes and coaches, at the 1972 Olympics in Munich, in which Eleven Israelis and one West German police officer were murdered, along with five of the eight assailants, due to a failed rescue mission is a case in point (Schiller and Young, 2010).

The violent attack on Sri Lanka's cricket team in the Pakistani city of Lahore in March 2009 caused the death of six police officers and two civilians (Shah and Pallister, 2009). Scientific analysis is needed in reporting such incidents as it exposed challenges of international communication on anti-terror strategies in the cricket field increased within and beyond the game, social caution, and the chaos in Pakistan.

The attack exposed human security menace in the Asian sub-continent, which had direct commercial and organizational effects on world cricket as several international teams refused to tour in Pakistan from 2001 onwards. India had to cancel a tour after the Islamic militant attacks on Mumbai in 2008, resulting in 164 deaths. After both attacks, the Indian Premier League (IPL) cricket tournament was transferred from India to South Africa due to security issues (direct effects on the tournament per se; the players; spectators; and national commercial sectors (Manthorp, 2009) (Wilson, 2009).

From a critical social scientific perspective, it is of crucial importance also to examine the debates and discourse of attackers identity. For Pakistani police, the main suspects were associates of banned Islamic groups with ties to Al Qaeda. However, speculation from police officers, terrorism experts, journalists, and Pakistani and Sri Lankan government ministers and officials pointed to a wide range of possible national and transnational backers for the attackers, including (in the most general terms) 'Indian hands' or the LTTE (Sri Lankan Tamil Tigers) (CNN-IBN, 2009; Thaindian News, 2009).

B. STATE DEVIANCE ON POPULATION

One of the major sports that unite states is football. Though international security trends expose have expose the vulnerability of mega sporting events, due to terrorism and jihadist tendencies. For example, in 1920, during the Irish war of independence, on 'Bloody Sunday', 14 British agents and auxiliaries were killed in Dublin by the Irish Republican Army; later that day, British troops fired on spectators at a Gaelic football match in Croke Park, with several casualties. This act by the by British forces provoked pro-Republican sentiments in Ireland. The incident was also commemorated in sport when the Hogan stand at Croke Park was so-named in honor of one Gaelic football player killed in the attack (Cronin, 1999).

A second instance is the 'Tlatelolco Massacre' in Mexico City, 1968, which occurred only 10 days prior to hosting the Olympic Games. A demonstration in Tlatelolco Square, in the capital's centre, appealing for socio-political change, turned violent with the Mexican army. A British sports journalist, Robert Trevor, recalls the incident: "When the helicopters opened fire and flares were dropped to light up the square, people were terrified. As we ran down the streets, we were met by Mexican soldiers in full battle order – steel helmets, rifles – and backed by armoured cars. People were being shot at from the front, by the foot soldiers, and from behind by the helicopter gunships, so they were trapped. It was terrible, and there was no escape" (BBC, 2008 online)

State responsibility is always put to question in relation to attacks perpetrated by jihadists and debates on social media sites and even television shows. Statesmen blame the demonstrators for provoking the police and causing the bloodshed. However, journalists in 2001 accessed official documents that revealed that Mexican security personnel had started the shooting, deliberately provoking the massacre (Economist, 2008a; Richman and Diaz-Cortes, 2008).

The era of state violence against civilian populations is sport venues is yet to be over. In Chile in the early 1970s, General Pinochet's military units and death squads detained, tortured and murdered thousands of opponents in the national stadium (Hachleitner, 2005).

In 1939, the Gestapo imprisoned some Jewish men in the Prater Stadium in Vienna. According to members of the anthropology department in Vienna's Natural History Museum, the men were deported to the Buchenwald concentration camp. Twenty-six men survived. One day after the deportation, a football match was staged in the stadium (Forster and Spring, 2008).

1. State Deviance in Africa: The Case of Guinea Conakry

In Guinea Conakry in 2009, a pro-democracy rally in the national football stadium led to a raid by security forces that fired on the crowd, leaving several casualties behind and women suffered systematic mass rapes by soldiers and police (Doyle, 2009). The Guinea military junta and police sought to mitigate the massacre, claiming few casualties, while attempting to bury the dead in secret mass graves. The United Nations and international NGOs argued that a case for 'crimes against humanity' should be pursued against those responsible (Human Rights Watch, 2009). However, in exploring the public meanings of terror, we may extend our constructivist approach in cultural anthropological terms, to explore how, at an everyday level, the meaning of the sports stadium is distorted, to become a site of terror, fear and anxiety; a labyrinthine space that provokes 'topophobia' rather than 'topophilia': that is, fear rather than a love of place (Bale, 1994; Eichberg, 1995).

2. Social Justice in the Sporting Milieu in Europe

In developed nations, it is possible to identify subtle interplays between the state, terrorism, discursive constructions, and social justice. We may consider, for example, how dominant forces within society extend the label 'terrorist' to encompass a broad range of perceived enemies. In the 1980s in the UK, the authoritarian New Right government under Margaret Thatcher reconfigured state institutions against 'internal enemies' which included paramilitary groups in Northern Ireland, football hooligans, the unemployed, and benefit claimants. Alongside non conventional actors who professed 'war' on football hooligans was waged at a number of levels: legal, through punitive sentencing and new laws, such as the Football Offences Act 1991, and the Football Disorder

Act 2000; bureaucratic, through more specialized policing frameworks, such as within the National Criminal Intelligence Service, which included a 'National Football Intelligence Unit' and other units investigating serious organized crime; bio-technological, through new security technologies and architectures to discipline and control inside stadiums; the strongest illustrations occurred inside stadiums, through all-seated stands (which served to pacify and to facilitate the monitoring of spectators), and CCTV systems.

French social theorist Jean Baudrillard (1993), English football hooliganism appears as the 'mirror of terrorism', which both dares the state to act while being a direct product of the state's callous social policies. Baudrillard examined the 1985 Heysel disaster as a form of 'hypermodern' terrorist event, wherein spectators intervene to take over from the football players as the main protagonists in the spectacle. The disaster occurred at the 1985 European Cup final, contested by Liverpool and Juventus at the Heysel Stadium in Brussels. Prior to kick-off, Liverpool fans charged at their Italian counterparts, who fled, leading to a collapsed wall due to crowd-crushing. Thirty-nine Juventus fans were fatally injured.

Meanwhile, the media is always ready to screen the disorder for a global audience. According to Baudrillard (1993: 79), hooligans are 'no different from terrorists', because they 'carry participation to its tragic limit, while at the same time daring the State to respond with violence, to liquidate them'. UK incident was considered a fatalistic response to Thatcher's administration, based on a draconian approach against 'unemployed hooligans', and other citizens believed to be marginalized violence inside stadiums.

Ironic interconnections between 'terrorists' and 'antiterrorist' strategies are increasingly linked to social

justice is their modus operandi. In research that would have intrigued Baudrillard, a report to Demos, the left-of-centre UK thinktank, identified a continuity between political and football 'terrorists', in that young Muslims who might have a potential propensity to violence were seen as having stronger parallels with football hooligans than with radical, peaceful Muslims (Bartlett et al., 2010).

Chapter Four

Jihadists Tendencies on Selected Soft Targets

Introduction

The 9/11 attacks did not only expose how globalized the world is, but also the menace on human security. Sovereignty free actors (al-Qaeda and ISIS) through several events have coordinated attacks at airplanes and airports, transportation systems such as buses and trains and even mega sporting events with huge crowds challenging international security norms. The jihadists also lunch cyber-attacks on some European websites, as well as organized operations on cartoonists satiric image of Prophet Muhammad.

Counterterrorism analysts subscribe to the fact that jihadists tendencies on locations such as airports, stadia and concert is to incite panic and fear within the population. Terrorism analyst Jessica Stern posed that, terrorists seek "to hit targets that will make us maximally afraid, and inflict the maximum amount of humiliation." Critical enough to explain the target selection for mass casualties such as clubs, cafes, and sporting events which are still feasible.

This chapter highlights not only the tactical considerations for target selection but also the ideological justifications. Analyzing al-Qaeda and ISIS's previous attacks in Mumbai, Nairobi and Paris, indicates the terrorists' theological and strategic justifications for specific targets.

Review of some selected Mass Casualty Urban Terrorist Assaults

ISIS is at the "cutting edge" of this type of mass casualty operations, with its "External Operations Department" in its sprawling Security Department ("Diwan al-Amn"). The agenda of this External Ops is to coordinate violent operations like mass casualty urban assaults in hostile territory. The "department" is made up of high-level planners, technocrats, bomb-makers, financiers, and combat units. The combat units have two divisions: well-trained individuals the suicide commandos with combat experience in Syria and Iraq. Inghimasi is ISIS assault or storm-troops (guerilla attack system) who attack fortified and defended positions.

The operational trends pose by a new subsect of terrorists is mass casualty urban terrorist attacks (MCUTA). However, this obstacle can be prevented or mitigated if known. Dealing MCUTA requires adequate intelligence with bilateral and multilateral coordination and cooperation. Terrorists who have done this in the past have committed appalling blunders that could have thwarted them and prevented large-scale mayhem and destruction.

Unfortunately, terrorist modus operandi seem to supersede that of the military. Each case in this study will proceed along the following lines: why was that particular city and country attacked; how did the attack proceed in terms of tactics, techniques and procedures and how did the government forces respond to the assault; and did the government have any prior warnings and indicators?

One of the case studies, Nairobi (2013), deals with a complex attack by heavily armed squads on a busy mall.

The other two attacks Mumbai (2008) and Paris (November 2015) were complex simultaneous attacks on soft targets (restaurants, bars, stadiums, concert hall, train station, religious centre, and hotels).

1. The Mumbai Assaults of 2008

November 26, 2008 terrorist attack in Mumbai has been termed India's 9/11 because of the mass casualties recorded. Complex attack within multiple locations for three days with international media coverage which Lashkar-e-Taiba (LeT), a radical Islamist terrorist group based in Pakistan, claimed responsibility for the attack.

The major question was, why Mumbai? Many Pakistan based terrorists see Hindu-majority India as an enemy of Islam. LeT had declared her agenda to spark chaos in India by an attack on Kashmir. That would exacerbate religious differences between India's Hindu majority and its Muslim community and facilitate the recruitment of new jihadists. As such an attack on Mumbai, India's commercial and entertainment centre, also considered "India's Wall Street, its Hollywood, and its Milan", was strategic to the group.

Taj Mahal Palace and Trident-Oberoi Hotels, which accommodated foreigners and local elites, was targeted by LeT for undertaking such an attack. This would help in gaining international propaganda to incite research on India's geopolitical trends. The Mumbai attacks appeal to conspiracy theories between LeT with the Inter-Services Intelligence (ISI) of a state sponsor, Pakistan. This was adequately exposed by an American prisoner David Headley. from prison claimed in the United States that there was coordination between ISI and LeT as he visited Mumbai on eight separate occasions to conduct a "recon" of the attack. His videos and map of the iconic Taj hotel were used to build up a mock-up for the assault team.

The planning for the attack began in 2006. LeT engaged in thorough preparation of the assault team, both physical and psychologically, in a training camp in Muzzaferabad in Pakistani, Kashmir. The terrorists were given pre-planned routes through the city from the point of their landing in Mumbai to their final terrain. The LeT trainers provided the jihadists with maps and images of their targets in a compact disc. Guided by their controllers in Pakistan, the trained terrorists made their way by sea from Pakistan, dissuaded Indian coastal patrols, and transferred from their vessels to an Indian fishing vessel which they captured and made their way into the fishing community Mumbai. Inadequate community policing made them gain grounds into the plan terrain in two different teams.

Inadequate cooperation and administrative visa are the aspects that limits counter-terrorism in some countries. In India, the various agencies involved in responding to jihadists tendencies were unable to collaborate with one another. Despite the number of terrorist attacks India has suffered over the years, Mumbai had not reinforced her security protocols to limit attacks on soft and hard targets.

More so, the Indian police squadron for strategic response to terrorism was not adequately trained and lack counterterrorism weaponry. There were tussles between the state in which Mumbai is located and the centre, New Delhi, over turf and who had authority over the response. Another challenge was the centrally controlled National Security Guards (NSG) with no orders to mobilize for hours and a lack of facilities like transportation for counterterrorism agents. The Mumbai attack is also noteworthy for the enormous amount of chatter it generated on jihadist websites. The discussion was mainly about the tactics, techniques and procedures of the terrorists and about the perceived weaknesses of the responding government agencies. One jihadist website, the al-Yaqin Media Center, released a study titled “The Mumbai Operations: A Study in the Local, Regional, and International Ramifications.” The study is worth examining in summary form as the author or authors were profoundly impressed by a number of factors ranging from the politico-strategic to the operational and tactical.

Information was available about the terrorists plan to attack Mumbai. In February 2008, a suspected terrorist arrested in northern India was found with drawings of various iconic sites in Mumbai, some of which were targets in the November 2008 attack. The suspect indicated that he had begun his reconnaissance in late 2007. Though India's Intelligence Bureau (IB), issued a warning that LeT had an interest in Mumbai and listed six potential targets of the group, it still happened.

By late October 2008, Great Britain and the United States also had intel, but they didn't share with India. The delays in intelligence sharing amongst the three countries ease the ‘game’. Great Britain had amassed considerable information about the online activities of one Zarrar Shah, the “technocrat” of LeT who was using Google Earth to map out the routes for the assault team from their landing site into the city and who was searching for “4 and 5 star” hotels in Mumbai. Indian's inadequate cooperation and due negligence of Britain on Shah's activities caused a major hit. The puzzle was because the three countries were not able to connect the dots by themselves and did not communicate and collaborate with one another.

2. The Assault on Westgate Mall, Nairobi 2013

Around 12:30 on Saturday, 21 September 2013, closed circuit television (CCTV) footage inside the Westgate Mall in Nairobi, Kenya exposed two gunmen entering the mall through the main entrance while two others made their way up a ramp to the rear parking deck. The Westgate mall is located in the affluent Westlands district of Nairobi, approximately 3.5 kilometres northwest of the city centre. The area is home to the capital's expatriate population, and the mall is popular with foreigners and middle-class Kenyans making it a lucrative target for the attackers.

The formal claim of responsibility issued by Al-Shabaab leader, Ahmed Abdi Godane, on 25 September 2013, stated that the Westgate attack was revenge for Kenya's policies, specifically as a legitimate response to Kenya's invasion of Somalia. Godane warned Kenyans "because it's you who have chosen your politicians...it's you who have supported your government's decision to go to war." Damaging its economy was a specific objective. Al-Shabaab claimed the attack was "a slap in the face of the dwindling economy of the Kenyan government," and warned that it would bring about Kenya's "economic downfall" if Kenyan forces failed to withdraw from Somalia.

Only three and half hours after the attack began, elements of the General Services Unit (GSU) "Recce Company" Kenya's internal anti-terrorism response force arrived at the Westgate Mall. GSU officers engaged the terrorists in a firefight and pinned them down inside the Nukumatt Store. Units of the Kenyan Army Ranger Regiment arrived and entered the mall. There was no command, coordination, and communication system between the police forces already there and the military units that came shortly thereafter. Even if it had been set up, it would not have made a difference as soldiers and police officers were equipped with incompatible radio systems. Little or no effort was made by members of the security forces to inform each other of planned assaults on the mall. This may be the reason why a "friendly fire" situation between Rangers/GSU and police occurred, claiming the life of one of the GSU "Recce Company" commanders and wounded three other GSU officers. At night, government forces lacking night vision gear, withdrew from the mall into perimeter positions. The militants appear to have used the confusion of the Kenyan forces to regroup and equip themselves with large-calibre weapons that had not featured in the initial phase of the attack. Government forces reported that the terrorists appeared to have hidden caches of ammunition and explosives inside the mall prior to the attack. The prepositioning of heavier weapons suggests that the militants anticipated a transition to a more defensive posture following their murderous spree.

Intelligence Breach

A year before, a Kenyan government intelligence report warned of a potential attack at Westgate. There were warnings that Al Shabaab intended to attack key targets in Nairobi. The briefing, dated 21 September 2012, assessed that the Somali terrorist organization, Al Shabaab, was planning to target the mall: "The following suspected Al Shabaab operatives are in Nairobi and are planning to mount suicide attacks on undisclosed date, targeting Westgate Mall." Another intelligence briefing warned of attacks like those that struck Mumbai in late 2008, "Where the operatives storm into a building with guns and grenades and probably hold hostages."

On 26 September 2013, Kenyan newspapers cited a leaked National Intelligence Service (NIS) report that revealed that the NIS had briefed ministers in January 2013 and again at the beginning of September, about terrorist plans to launch simultaneous terrorist attacks in Nairobi and Mombasa around September. The NIS warned that Al Shabaab was planning to carry out suicide attacks on targets, including the Westgate Mall. Another report even named the eventual target, stating, "The following suspected Al Shabaab operatives are in Nairobi and are planning to mount suicide attacks.

The leaks of the 32-page intelligence file, obtained by Al Jazeera, suggested five senior officials including the secretaries of interior, defence, foreign affairs, and treasury, as well as the chief of defence forces was aware of imminent threats. The senior officials were briefed on the "noticeable rise in the level of threat" starting on 13 September, eight days before the Westgate attack. Several security analysts told Al Jazeera that institutional rivalry and unclear command lines within Kenyan security agencies were the likely reasons behind the failure to foil the Westgate strike. The Kenyan intelligence service has become politicized and appears to be more focused on neutralizing political opponents rather than protecting the country from internal and external aggression. The mall attack and its aftermath has deepened Kenya's ethnic and political divisions, fomenting unrest in a country long seen as an icon of stability in increasingly volatile East Africa.

3. Paris Attacks of November 2015

The Paris attack of November 2015 recorded several casualties. Attacks perpetrated by several terrorists using automatic weapons and explosives evading a number of locations, including a stadium, a concert hall, restaurant and bars at the same time (BBC: 2015). According to BBC, an attacker screamed "God is great" in Arabic: this was believed to be the first proof of a terrorist attack. The attack redefined French counter terrorism approach, since events took place in the presence of President Francoise Hollande. The president described the attacks as an act of war planned by the Islamic State (BBC: 2015).

a) Football Stadium

The recovery strategy started immediately as the attacks were taking place in several locations. The president was informed and taken to safety. At that particular moment, he was in one of the targeted locations in the Stade de France. The stadium was being targeted from outside and three explosions detonated at 9.20 pm, 9.30 pm and 9.53 pm local time during a friendly football match between Germany and France. At the moment, 80.000 sports fans had no idea about the attack believing the attack to be fireworks. At the end of the match fans gathered on the pitch since only three exits were open. (The Guardian: 2015). President Hollande convened an emergency cabinet meeting with Prime Minister Manuel Valls and Interior Minister Bernard Cazaneuve (BBC: 2015). As a consequence, stronger border controls were introduced and a state of emergency inside the country was declared.

In addition, highly trained security forces were ordered to enter the Bataclan concert venue, one of the attack premises, which were a concert hall, managing to kill one of three terrorists. It is believed that the terrorist attacked in three teams. In addition to the three terrorists at the Bataclan concert venue, three terrorists detonated themselves outside the Stade de France, another terrorist died using the same method at the Comptoir Voltaire cafe on the Boulevard Voltaire (BBC: 2015).

The crisis was still ongoing as the whole city, country and world were in a state of shock and paralyzed (BBC: 2015). The city was placed on lockdown, parts of the metro, schools and several tourists locations e.g. Eiffel tower were closed down (BBC: 2015). In the days to follow French policemen were ordered to raid various locations throughout the country in order to search and find suspects. (BBC: 2015) One of these raids was conducted in the Saint Denis area of

Paris where the attack organizer Abdelhamid Abaaoud was shot together with another terrorist. This raid is believed to have avoided another imminent attack (BBC: 2015). Abdelhamid Abaaoud was a Belgian national and was raised in Molenbeek, a poor district with high unemployment with a majority of Arab immigrant population. He, as well as the other terrorist believed to have been recruited by the Islamic State militant group (IS) (BBC: 2015). The French Interior Minister said their operation plan was always equal, attacks were prepared from the exterior by jihadists with a European passport, who were trained and then returned to the EU to execute an attack (BBC: 2015).

b) Headquarters of the satirical magazine Charlie Hebdo in Paris

On 7 January 2015, three gunmen of the jihadist movement Daesh, broke into the headquarters of the satirical magazine Charlie Hebdo in Paris, France and assassinated 11 members of its editorial committee. France went on her knees after the incident, which she had not encountered for more than half a century. This fact was superseded on 13 November when eight terrorist operatives, equipped with assault rifles and suicide vests, divided into three teams and simultaneously stunned restaurants, bars, a sports arena and a concert venue, all within a 3 km radius in Paris. The remaining group shot 39 people at three different restaurants in the fashionable east district of Paris. Over three hours, 130 people were killed, including 89 at the Bataclan theatre following a three-hour hostage standoff, with over 350 injured.

Prior to these attacks, concerns for public safety were already high due to the Charlie Hebdo attack earlier in the year. Meanwhile, France continued to support military strikes against Syria and Iraq, whilst disenfranchised youth of North African descent found solidarity and a sense of belonging within the Jihadi cells expanding in the country. As the terror unfolded on 13 November, stunned Parisians and French residents together with rest of the world, watched on and reached out via social media to share, condone and mourn. Local residents via twitter and Facebook, offered shelter to those civilians trapped on the streets of Paris, who now found themselves in the wrong place at the wrong time. Muslim organizations across France, such as the Union of Islamic Organizations of France, condemned the attacks in Paris, which consequently impacted Muslim-owned businesses. Parisian residents were also concerned the attacks may lead to a marginalization of Muslims in the city.

France has always been of particular interest for jihadist terrorists. ISIS seems to have a particular hatred for France, made very clear in a French-language article entitled "L' Histoire de l'Inimite de France envers l'Islam" or the History of French Hatred of Islam. The article describes the days of the first Crusades (1096- 1099) when the French Pope Urban II urged the nobles of France to go "fight Islam" in the Holy Land. For ISIS, France's secular and democratic values were anathema as was its presence in the Middle East and North Africa where it was first a colonial power and later, provided support to local governments fighting extremists.

France's military was already involved in airstrikes against ISIS positions in Syria before the November 2015 terrorist attack. Why was a large-scale attack like this, which would have a pre-operational footprint, not picked up by the intelligence services? The intelligence services in France and Belgium knew about the suspects' backgrounds. Five had travelled to fight in Syria and returned to France or Belgium. One of the attackers at the Stade de France, Omar Ismail Mostefai, had a French police "S" file indicating suspected radicalization since 2010. He had gone to Syria in 2013 and returned to France in the spring of 2014. Sami Amimour, one of the gunmen at the Bataclan, had been detained in October 2012 on suspicion of terrorist links, and had an international arrest warrant and yet was able to travel to Syria in 2013. He returned in mid-October 2014, and was able to evade surveillance and apprehension until the attacks. Salah Abdeslam, who took on a logistics role, is the brother of one of the terrorists who blew himself up outside the Comptoir Voltaire café. Salah Abdeslam was stopped on the French-Belgian border a few hours after the attack and questioned but then released. He was only apprehended in late March 2016 in Molenbeek, a Brussels suburb, because he made the mistake of using a mobile that was being tracked by the authorities.

François Heisbourg, a former member of a French presidential commission of defense and security, and one of Europe's leading strategic thinkers argued that the biggest problem was not a shortage of information about suspects but a lack of capacity to process that information. It was less a failure of intelligence than the ability to follow through on the intelligence data. The terrorists were giving off signals but the French security and intelligence services were inundated with information and were unable to connect the dots. Failure to analyze the information was not the only problem. French intelligence faces a problem created by the gap between available personnel and the huge number of suspects.

Chapter Five

Counterterrorism on Soft Targets: Russia as Case Study

Introduction

There exist several methods for conflict resolution; mediation, negotiation and arbitration amongst states or parties engaged. Sports is a strategic tool uses for reconciliation in the world. In organizational research, strategy defines the pattern through which entities respond to external threats and opportunities based on its resources and capabilities. In 2017, Hamming published a guided on coordinated attacks and plots in the West. His works were used in analyzing attacks between 2010 and 2017, demonstrate AQ and IS's coordinated attacks as well organized networks; while IS coordinated 38 attacks, AQ perpetrated a total of 11.

Terrorism is a polemical word that has long provoked interpretation discrepancies worldwide. Although there are different reasons hindering international consensus, subjectivity remains a major obstacle in defining the term. Walter Laqueur and Bruce Hoffman counterterrorism experts elaborated on certain points which are adequate in defining terrorism. In addition to its aspiration for power (political) and use of violence, there are some major criteria for describing contemporary terrorism.

1. It is about power: Terrorists want power; terrorism is designed to create power where there is none or to consolidate it where there is very little.
2. It is systematic: The terrorist enterprise is a planned, calculated, and indeed systematic act. Terrorism is a method, rather than a set of adversaries or the causes they pursue.
3. It is designed to have the ripple effect of fear: Terrorism seeks to go beyond the immediate target victims; it seeks to have far-reaching psychological repercussions.
4. It is non-state: Terrorism is more usefully regarded as a most serious breach of peace in which non-state entities participate. Today it is usually a networked, leaderless adversary, either a subnational group or non-state entity, ideologically motivated.
5. It is rational: The terrorist strives to act optimally in order to achieve his goal in a clear demonstration of an entirely rational choice, often reluctantly embraced after considerable reflection and debate, weighing costs and benefits before undertaking the murderous journey.

Russian Grand Strategy in Countering Attacks on Soft Targets

President Obama's "Yes We Can" is a formidable tag to brandish the Russian Federation flag, following her demarcation in counter-terrorism. The FIFA World Cup 2018 in Russia changed expose new counter-terrorism techniques to the world. Cyber defence force readily armed to destroy any flying bird, intelligence agency well structures and booking of tickets, well organized after profiling the individual either tourist or participant in the competition.

The Russian Deputy Prime Minister Vitaly Mutko boasted of the multiple security measures adopted for hard and soft targets in order to sustain tourists visiting the country during the event. Russia security adviser and counter-terrorism unit analyzed the modus operandi of the 1972 Munich Olympics attack, the 2013 Boston Marathon, and the November 2015 attack outside the Stade de France in Paris by an Islamic State cell based in Belgium, to develop an appropriate counter-terrorism strategy for the event.

During the 2017 Confederations Cup in Russia, the Federal Security Service (FSB) reportedly spotted a jihadi terrorist move on a high-speed train between Moscow and St. Petersburg. The aspirants intended to crash two express trains close to St. Petersburg. An Uzbek Islamic State leader Hamza, based in Kunduz, told Al Jazeera in 2017 about Islamic State in Khorasan, an Afghan-Pakistan affiliation of Islamic State aspiring to attack Russia. They boasted to Al Jazeera, "We have 4,000 trained fighters at the ready. God willing, 2,000 of them will go on the offensive against Russia." Though a terrorist cell leader declared, "With God's help, some of our forces have already entered Russia and we plan to send more." Another said, "They (the Russians) are at war with us, engaging us on the air and the ground".

Russian's counter-terrorism method in the Middle East, particularly in Syria threatened jihadi ideology of Islam and the Holy Quran (mujahidin). Response why Russia is amongst jihadists targets, as Pro-Islamic State platforms continue post threatening videos about her. For example, the pro-Islamic State Wafa' Media Foundation shared a series of online propaganda posters, one of which exposed a jihadi equipped with a bomb staring at a soccer stadium, emblazoned with the words "O enemies of Allah in Russia. I swear the mujahedeen fire will burn you. Just you wait."

Moreover, threatening image was released on the encrypted app Telegram by terrorists in April 2018 stating; "Russia 2018. Putin you disbeliever. You will pay the price for killing Muslims." On the right side of the image, a bearded jihadi was brandishing an AK47 assault rifle, emerging from an explosion in front of a packed soccer arena. The left side of the poster was Putin with his entire body trapped in the crosshairs of a jihadi's rifle.

In 2018, a poster designed by al-Nur Media Center (an Islamic State-linked French media group) and published on Telegram, terrorists sent a message to aspirants and armchair jihadists. The image showed flags of countries competing in the FIFA World Cup with the French text "Choisis ta Cible" (Choose your Target). One soccer star identified kneeling down in Moscow's Luzhniki Stadium, with an orange jumpsuit next to a masked jihadi, the field preview for the world cup final. Later, the Islamic State produced a graphic depicting a camouflaged terrorist outside of a stadium stadium armed with a gun and explosives

Russian Counter-Terrorism Mechanism

Russia is changing the dynamics of counter-terrorism in the world, from the Middle East to Europe and now extending support to Africa in the fight against terrorist organizations like Boko-Haram. In 2018, Islamic State aspirations to perpetrate profile attacks in Moscow were countered by Russia. Though the FSB attest of countering a four-man Islamic State sleeper cell, with command line in Syria using Telegram messenger service, a journal flag Russian counterterrorism agents arresting alleged Islamic State members, also figure in Western media, where a "shooting robot" neutralized the threat from an Islamic State-linked cell in Dagestan.

Igor Kulyagin, head of Russian National Anti-Terrorism Committee reported that: "We have taken into account the huge experience, accumulated by the National AntiTerrorism Committee and the security organizations involved in providing security for the Sochi Olympic Games, the Kazan Universiade and other huge events … Of course, special attention will be paid to providing anti-terrorism safeguards of the infrastructure that will be used for hosting the competition, such as the teams' stadiums, accommodation units and training facilities."

Sergei Umnov, the head of Russia's Ministry of Internal Affairs in St. Petersburg, sought to mitigate fears of terror attacks, exposing on the security protocols which will be carried out on a daily basis, 11,000 people will be working; 4,500 security agents will be coordinating activities in the city (St. Petersburg) in order for sustainable peace. Volunteers and private security organization will engage community policing. Russian official acknowledged adequate security protocol during the 2014 Sochi Winter Olympics, which became known as the "Security Olympics" for the massive security presence, as a testament for counterterrorism.

However, identifying and recognizing the grievances of a particular terrorist group is essential for intelligence agencies in analyzing the tenacity of their deeds. The transportation networks between cities, including trains, buses, and airplanes, will also be vulnerable, not forgetting stadiums and shopping malls. The Russian Federation grand strategy to combat terrorism is well known, despite the protein alliance with the Syrian regime. To secure the event in such diverse and dangerous regions, the Russian government implemented rigorous anti-terror measures during the event:

1. Total bans on planes and 'flying devices,' such as drones, around World Cup stadiums
2. Stringent ID checks ensuring that the identity of fans is known in advance

3. Road closure and high security on train and planes transporting teams between match venues

Russia's Anti-Terrorism Committee allocated financial resources to strengthen her security system, focusing on airports and transport hubs. Facial recognition technology with cross-matched with images of wanted individuals from across government databases and social media, were also installed on 5,000 CCTV cameras across Moscow. Other host cities were equipped with CCTV cameras connected to security database.

Spectators were given FAN-IDs, as a sort of identification information used by Russian security services for vetting. The Russian Tass News Agency reported that security will be maintained at the World Cup venues by 14,500 security guards and 16,500 stewards. Stadiums in the 11 cities hosting matches will have high-tech security systems that include super-sensitive metal detectors at all steel-gated entry checkpoints. As non-conventional actors aspire to attack strategic areas search conducted by guards using handheld scanners will draw the population closer, when a terrorist start posing problems before detonating a bomb. Bombsniffing dogs, and bags been passed through airport-style X-ray machines may be suitable but not quite adequate. "Electronic warfare assets" will be deployed to protect stadiums from hostile drones.

The Arab Spring, which had already led to the downfall of the governments of four countries before allowing the Islamic State to take root in Syria, is only part of the context for historical facts. The question is how much damage the Islamic State will be able to inflict before been eradicated. Military action will limit its physical reach but will not destroy its ideology, either in Iraq and Syria or further afield, unless there is something available to take its place 'education'.

Beyond that is the globalization era marked with increasing security trends within and out communities. The question is how much damage the Islamic State will be able to inflict before been eradicated. Military action will limit its physical reach but will not destroy its ideology, either in Iraq and Syria or further afield, unless there is something available to take its place 'education'.

Conclusion

As terrorist aspire to stage humiliating attacks on states notably on soft targets, cooperation should be the major tool for counter terrorism agencies with other security departments and experts. One of the worst tools in the field of counter terrorism is the hand metal detector. The aim of jihadists is mass casualty, panic and history. When a suspected terrorist or jihadist approaches a security agent holding a metal detector in a crowded environment, he (terrorist) creates a situation which will gather the population around him before he detonates a bomb. Terrorists also derive several ways to bypass this security checks; for the events of the Stade de Paris expose how vulnerable French citizens are to the new world order, with coordinated attacks claimed by ISIS.

Moreover, the method of evacuation in case of an attack on a stadium for spectators demurs a strategic challenge. Terrorist organizations through their technocrats (hackers, computer programmers and network analyst) may breach system of the sporting avenue in order to draw their target to a suitable zone of the attack. Their hackers interfere in communication network, redirect images of CCTV camera which facilitates the perpetration of an attack. Security system of sporting avenues should be secured by counter-terrorism agency in collaboration with special unit of operation known to the presidency.

In addition to the above, counter-terrorism agencies need to cooperate in order to curb this global menace. Intelligence is sensitive issue in terms of counter-terrorism; as such the breach of the Nigeria Secret Service database in 2012 is critical for her present geopolitical situation, with the development of alliances (Boko-Haram and Islamic State) with the region will only plunge the world in chaos. This is because strategic institution likes the Nigerian Secret Service as example, which server have maps of strategic buildings in the country and vital data about international and national persons, security codes or protocols can be exploited by terrorist to access certain infrastructures. Counter-terrorism is not only limited to civil-military relations, intelligence sharing, but also community policing

Bibliography

Articles and Journals

Abdullahi, Y. (2016) Reflection on the Intellectual Legacy of the Sokoto Jihad. World Scientific News 32 (2016) 95-105

Abraham Pizam, Ginger Smith (2000) Tourism and Terrorism: A Historical Analysis Of Major Terrorism Acts And Their Impact On Tourism Destinations, Tourism Economics, Vol. 6, No. 2, (2000), pp. 123-138.

Ahmed, A. 2002. Ibn Khaldun's understanding of civilizations and the dilemmas of Islam and the West today. Middle East Journal 56:20-45.

Ajayi, J.F.A (1965), 'West Africa states at the beginning of the Ninetieth Century', in J.F.A. Ajayi, and E. Ian, (eds.) A thousand years of West African History. Ibadan: Ibadan University Press, pp. 253266.

Al-Amarah, L.M. (2009). Russian strategy in the post-Cold War and its repercussions in the Arab region. CAUS.

Al Arabiya 20th September 2013, Tunisia says sexual jihadist girls returned home from Syria pregnant

http://english.alarabiya.net/en/variety/2013/09/20/Tunisia-says-sexual-jihadist-girls-returned-home-fromSyria-pregnant.html

Asma Barlas's; Jihad, Holy War, and Terrorism: The Politics of Conflation and Denial

Asseburg, M., & Wimmen, H. (2016). Dynamics of transformation, elite change and new social mobilization in the Arab World. Mediterranean Politics, 21, (1), 1-22. https://doi.org/10.1080/13629395.2015.1081448

Aymennal Tamimi http://www.ecfr.eu/content/entry/commentary_the_islamic_states_regional_strategy 32646

Bartlett J, Birdwell J and King M (2010) The Edge of Violence. London: Demos.

Baudrillard J (1993) The Transparency of Evil. London: Verso.

BBC News, (2015), Paris attacks: What happened on the night? http://www.bbc.co.uk/news/world-europe-34818994 (Accessed December 15, 2015)

Bohlen, C. (2016) Parisians fear terror attacks will divide, not unite, the city. Available at: http://www.nytimes.com/2015/11/15/world/europe/parisians-fear-attacks-will-divide-not-unite-the-city.html?rref=collection%2Fnewseventcollection%2Fattacksinparis &action=click&contentCollection=europe&region=rank&module= package&version=highlight&contentPlacement=2&pgtype= collection&_r=0 (Accessed: 3 October 2016).

Boyle P and Haggerty KD (2009) Spectacular security: Mega-events and the security complex. Political Sociology 3: 257–274.

Bristow M (2008) China's Olympic security dilemma. BBC News, 12 March, available at: http:// news.bbc.co.uk/2/hi/asia-pacific/7292025.stm (accessed 20 January 2011).

Brown, N. J. 1997. Shari'a and state in the modern Muslim Middle East. International Journal of Middle East Studies 29:359-376.

Castillo, M., Haddad, M., Martinez, M. and Almasy, S. (2015) Paris suicide bomber identified; ISIS claims responsibility for 129 dead. Available at: http://edition.cnn.com/2015/11/14/world/paris-attacks/ (Accessed: 5 October 2016).

Clemenceau F., 2015. Pas de victoire à court terme, Le Journal du Dimanche, 22 November.

CNN-IBN (2009) Lankan group behind SL cricket team attack: Pak, 6 September, available at: http://ibnlive.in.com/news/lankan-group-behind-sl-cricket-team-attack-pak/100794-2.html (accessed 20 January 2011).

Cohen, A. (2007). Putin's Middle East visit: Russia is back. The Heritage Foundation. Retrieved from https://www.heritage.org/europe/report/putins-middle-east-visit-russia-back

Collin, K. (2018, March 16). 7 years into the Syrian war, is there a way out? Brookings. Retrieved from https://www.brookings.edu/blog/order-from-chaos/2018/03/16/7-yearsinto-the-syrian-war-is-there-a-way-out/

De Vreese, Stephan. 2000. "Hooliganism Under the Statistical Magnifying Glass: A Belgian Case Study." European Journal on Criminal Policy and Research 8: 201-23.

Donnan, H. Editor. 2002. Interpreting Islam. London: SAGE.

Doyle M (2009) Unearthing the truth of Guinea 'bloodbath'. BBC News, 25 November, available at: http://news.bbc.co.uk/1/hi/8376800.stm (accessed 20 January 2011).

Economist (2008a) The ghosts of Mexico 1968. A massacre that was hushed up to ensure a 'successful' sporting event, 24 April. Available at: http://www.economist.com/node/11090825 (accessed 20 January 2011).

Elliott, C. (2015, November) What We Got Right And Wrong In Coverage Of The Paris Attacks. The Guardian. Retrieved from: Https://Www.Theguardian.Com/Commentisfree/2015/ Nov/23/What-We-Got-Right-And-Wrong-Incoverage-Of-The-Paris-Attacks

Ewen MacAskill, "How French intelligence agencies failed before the Paris attacks," The Guardian, 19 November 2015, http://www.theguardian.com/world/2015/nov/19/howfrench-intelligence-agencies-failed-before-the-paris-attacks

Fox, J. 2001. Two Civilizations and Ethnic Conflict: Islam and the West. Journal of Peace Research 38:459-472.

Gilsenan, M. 1990a. Recognizing Islam: Religion and Society in the Modern Middle East. London: I.B. Tauris.

Giulianotti, R. and Klauser, F. (2012) Sport mega-events and 'terrorism': A critical analysis. International Review for the Sociology of Sport June 47, issue 3, 307-323, 2012

G. Wood, What ISIS Really Wants, The Atlantic, 2017, https://www.theatlantic.com/magazine/archive/2015/03/what-isis-really-wants/384980/

Halliday, F. 1999. Review article: 'Islamophobia' reconsidered. Ethnic and Racial Studies 22:892-902.

Hassan Abu Hanieh, Divergence of the Syrian Conflict: The Disease of Sectarianism. http://arabi21.com/story/725770/%D8%A7%D9%86%D8%AD%D8%B1%D8%A7%D9%81 12 F. Gregory Gause, III. Beyond

Hassan Abu Hanieh, The Islamic State's Media Apparatus: The Caliphate's Electronic Army. http://arabi21.com/story/803770/%D8%A7%D9%84%D8%A2%D9%84%D8%A9-

How ISIS leader Abu Bakr al-Baghdadi became the world's most powerful jihadist leader http://www.washingtonpost.com/news/43 morning-mix/wp/2014/06/11/how-isis-leader-abu-bakr-al-baghdadi-became-the-worlds-most-powerful-jihadi-leader/

How an arrest in Iraq revealed Isis's $2bn jihadist network http://www.theguardian.com/world/2014/jun/15/iraq-isis-arrest-84 jihadists-wealth-power.

ISIS breach of Iraq-Syria border merges two wars into one 'nightmarish reality' http://www.theguardian.com/world/2014/jun/18/47 isis-iraq-syria-two-wars-one-nightmare.

Islamic State, I Jane's 360, Jane's World Insurgency and Terrorism http://www.janes.com/security/ terrorism-insurgency

Issue 3 of Dabiq was titled 'A Call to Hijra' (migration) and much of its content was aimed at persuading new recruits to join the 119 State.

Ken Dilanian, Islamic State Group's War Chest Is Growing Daily, The Big Story, 15 September 2014, http://Bigstory.Ap.Org/Article/Islamic-State-Groups-War-Chest-Growing-Daily-0

Moeller, H.M. (2016) Why soft target terrorist attacks will remain a threat | GRI. Available at: http://globalriskinsights.com/2016/07/soft-target-terrorist-attacks/ (Accessed: 30 September 2016).

On-Field Sports Spectatorship And Patronage: A Sociological Xray Of Its Determinants For Effective Sports Management In Developing Countries by Elendu Ifeanyichukwu Christian and Okafor Christopher Obiora. British Journal of Education, Vol.6, No.2, pp.84-93, February 2018. www.eajournals.org

P. Holtmann, Terrorism and Jihad: Differences and Similarities, in "Perspectives on Terrorism", Vol. 8, No. 3, 2014. http://www.terrorismanalysts.com/pt/index.php/pot/article/view/352/html

Rethinking Pre-Colonial State Formation and Ethno-Religious Identity Transformation in Hausaland under the Sokoto Caliphate By Lenshie, Nsemba Edward & Ayokhai, F.E.F. Global Journal of HUMAN SOCIAL SCIENCE Political Science Volume 13 Issue 4 Version 1.0 Year 2013

Russett, B. M., J. R. Oneal, and M. Cox. 2000. Clash of civilizations, or realism and liberalism déjà vu? Some evidence. Journal of Peace Research 37:583-608.

Russia in the Middle East: Back to a "Grand strategy" – or enforcing Multilateralism? By Ekaterina Stepanova. politique étrangère 2:2016

Sabet, A. G. E. 2000. Feature review: The end of fundamentalism? Third World Quarterly 21:891-902.

Sadiki, L. 2000. Popular uprisings and Arab democratisation. International Journal of Middle East Studies 32:71-95.

Sebastian Rotella, James Glanz, and David Sanger, "In 2008 Mumbai Attacks, Piles of Spy Data, but Uncompleted Puzzle," New York Times, 21 December 2014, http://www.nytimes.com/2014/12/22/world/asia/in-2008-mumbai-a

Shah S and Pallister D (2009) Pakistan police claim arrests over gun attack on Sri Lankan cricket team. The Guardian, 4 March, available at: http://www.guardian.co.uk/world/2009/mar/04/ nglish-srilanka (accessed 20 January 2011).

Smith, Mike (2016). Boko Haram. Inside Nigeria's Unholy War. London: I.B. Tauris & Co. p. 32-52

Sunni rebels declare new 'Islamic caliphate' http://www.aljazeera.com/news/ middleeast/2014/06/isil-declares-new-islamic-17 caliphate-201462917326669749.html

Tal Koren and Gabi Siboni, 'The Caliphate' extends into Facebook: How does 'Da'esh' recruit new jihadists in cyberspace? http://www.rcssmideast.org/Article/2654/%D9%83%D9%8A%D9%81%D8%AA%D8%AC%D9%86%D8%AF

Thaindian News (2009) Indian hand in Sri Lankan cricket team attack: Pakistan, 10 April. Available at: http://www.thaindian.com/newsportal/india-news/nglis-hand-in-sri-lankan-cricket-teamattack-pakistan_100178135.

The Islamic State: Between Truth and Illusion, Mansour Abu Abdullah Mohamed, Dar al-Jabiya, 2014.

"The Islamic State: from Baghdadi the founder to Baghdadi the caliph" http://english.al-akhbar.com/node/20599

The Kerslake Report: An independent review into the preparedness for, and emergency response to, the Manchester Arena attack on 22nd May 2017

Turki al-Jasser, "What Do Young People Find Enticing About ISIL?" http://altagreer.com/%D9%85%D8%A7%D8%A7%D9%84%D8%B0%D9%8A%D9%8A%D8%AC%D8%A8%D8%A3%D9%86%D8%AA%D8%B9%D8%B1%D9%81%D9%87%D8%B9%D9%86%D8%A8%D8%B1

%D9%86%D8%A7%D9%85%D8%AC%D9%88%D9%83%D8%A7%D9%84%D8%A9%D8%A7%D9%84%D8%A3/

William Rosenau, "Every room is a new battle:" The lessons of modern urban warfare," Studies in Conflict and Terrorism, Vol. 20, No. 4 (1997),pp. 373-374.

Institutions

Aaron Y. Zelin, Sunni Foreign Fighters in Syria: Background, Facilitating Factors, and Select Responses. http://www.washingtoninstitute.org/ar/policy-analysis/view/sunni-foreign-fighters-insyria-background-facilitating-factors-and-select

Ahmed, H. (2016) Cities under Siege: Mass Casualty Urban Terrorism Assaults. S. Rajaratnam School of International Studies (RSIS) on 5 May 2016.

Alexander Meindl (2018) The Impacts of Terrorism on Tourism in the EU, Bachelor Thesis at Modul Vienna University, Private University.

Alterman, J., & Todman, W. (2018). The implications of the US withdrawal from Syria. Center for Strategic & International Studies. Retrieved from https://www.csis.org/ analysis/implications-us-withdrawal-syria

"Al-Yaqin Media Center Releases Analysis of Mumbai Attacks," Open Source CenterGMP20090209386004, 6 January 2009,https://www.opensource.gov/portal/server.pt/ gateway/PTARGS_0_0_200_240_1019_43/h

Beckett, T. (2018, October 23). Tactics before strategy: understanding today's Middle East. International Institute for Strategic Studies. Retrieved from https://www.iiss.org/blogs/analysis/2018/10/todays-middle-east

Changes in modus operandi of Islamic State Terrorist Attacks, Europol Public Information

Charlie Winter, The Virtual 'Caliphate': Understanding Islamic State's Propaganda Strategy, Quilliam Foundation, July 2015 http://www.quilliamfoundation.org/ wp/wpcontent/uploads/publications/free/thevirtual-caliphate- understanding-islamic-states-propaganda-strategy.pdf (Retrieved on 14 November 2015).

CONNABLE, B., & WASSER, B. (2018). The limits of Russian strategy in the Middle East. The London School of Economics and Political Science. Retrieved from https://blogs.lse.ac.uk/mec/2018/05/09/the-limits-of-russian-strategy-in-the-middle-east/

Hamas. 1988. The Covenant of the Islamic Resistance Movement. Available: www.yale.edu/lawweb/avalon/mideast/hamas.htm Accessed: 22 January 2003.

Home Office (2010) Olympic cyber security plan to be developed, 25 November. Available at: http://www.homeoffice.gov.uk/media-centre/news/English-cyber (accessed 20 January 2011).

Home Office. 2004. "Home Office Statistics on Football-Related Arrests and Banning Orders: Season 2003/2004." Retrieved October 2, 2010 (http://www. homeoffice.gov.uk/documents/football -arrests-03042835.pdf? view¼ Binary).

Home Office. 2005. "Home Officc Statistics on Football-Related Arrests and Banning Orders: Season 2004/2005." Retrieved October 2, 2010 (http:// www.home office.gov.uk/documents/football _Arrest_BO_2004-52835.pdf? view¼Binary).

Home Office. 2006. "Home Office Statistics on Football-Related Arrests and Banning Orders: Season 2005/2006." Retrieved October 2, 2010 (http://www. homeoffice.gov.uk/documents/football -arrests-05062835.pdf?view¼Binary).

Home Office. 2007 "Home Office Statistics on Football-Related Arrests and Banning Orders: Season 2006/2007." Retrieved October 2, 2010 (http://www.home office.gov.uk/documents/football -arreststatistics-20072835.pdf?view¼Binary).

Home Office. 2008 "Home Office Statistics on Football-Related Arrests and Banning Orders: Season 2007/2008." Retrieved October 2, 2010 (http://www. homeoffice.gov.uk/documents/football -arrests-07082835.pdf?view ¼Binary).

Home Office. 2009. "Home Office Statistics on Football-Related Arrests and Banning Orders: Season 2008/2009." Retrieved October 2, 2010 (http:// www.homeoffice.gov.uk/documents/football -arrests-08092835.pdf?view¼Binary).

Human Rights Watch (2009) Bloody Monday: The September 28 Massacre and Rapes by Security Forces in Guinea. New York: Human Rights Watch.

ISIS Annual Report Reveal A Metrics-Driven Military Command http://www.understandingwar.org/backgrounder/ 99 ISIS-Annual-Reports-Reveal-Military-Organization.

ISIS Governance in Syria, Charles Caris and Samuel Reynolds, the Institute for the Study of War, July 2014. http://49 www.understandingwar.org/sites/default/files/ISIS_Governance.pdf.

ISIS AND PROPAGANDA: HOW ISIS EXPLOITS WOMEN by Mah-Rukh Ali. Reuters Institute Fellowship Paper University of Oxford

Katz, M.(2010). Russia's greater Middle East policy: Securing economic interests, courting Islam. IFRI. Retrieved from https://www.ifri.org/sites/default/files/atoms/files/ifrirussiamiddleeastkatzengapril2010.pdf

Kelly, S.; Asante, S.; Jung, J. C. D.; Kesaite, V.; Woo, G.; A Risk Analysis Retrospective on the 2015 Paris Attacks; Working Paper 2016:1; Cambridge Risk Framework series; Centre for Risk Studics; University of Cambridge.

Kelly, S.; Jung, J. C. D.; Kesaite, V.; Woo, G.; 2015 Paris Attacks: A Risk Perspective; Working Paper 2015:1; Cambridge Risk Framework series; Centre for Risk Studies; University of Cambridge.

Magen, Z. (2016). How deep are the cracks in the Russian-Iranian coalition in Syria? INSS Insight, no. 783. The Institute for National Security Studies. Retrieved from http://www.inss.org.il/publication/how-deep-are-the-cracks-in-the-russian-iranian-coalitionin-syria/

Maha Yahya, Fatal Attraction: Five Reasons Young People Join 'Da'esh'. http://carnegiemec.org/publications/?fa=57251

Political Islam in the Middle East by Are Knudsen, Chr. Michelsen Institute Development Studies and Human Rights. www.cmi.no/public/public.htm

Report of the Secretary-General on the threat posed by ISIL (Da'esh) to international peace and security and the range of United Nations efforts in support of Member States in countering the threat, United Nations Security Council, S/2016/92, 29 January 2016.

Richard Barrett, The Islamic State, The Soufan Group, November 2014.

Sectarianism: The New Middle East Cold War. Brookings Doha Center Analysis Paper, Number 11, July 2014. http://www.brookings.edu/~/media/research/files/papers/2014/07/22-beyond-sectarianismcold-war-gause/arabic-pdf.pdf

Stepanova, E. (2018). Russia and conflicts in the Middle East: Regionalization and implications for the West. The International Spectator, 53(4), 35-57 . https://doi.org/10.1080/ 03932729.2018.1507135

The Evolution of Jihadi Terrorism from al-Qaeda to Daesh by Francesco Farinelli (EFD – European Foundation for Democracy) inThe Evolution Of Jihadist Radicalization In Asia

The Islamic State By Richard Barrett. The Soufan Group, November 2014

"The Lessons of the Mumbai Attack," RAND

The Peace Alliance, Global terrorism index release; insights on Paris & other global attacks (2016) , http://www.peacealliance.org/globalterrorism-index-release-insights-on-paris-other-global-attacks

Yezid Sayigh, ISIS: Global Islamic Caliphate or Islamic Mini-State in Iraq? http://carnegieendowment.org/2014/07/24

Books

Geertz, C. 1973. "Religion as a cultural system," in The Interpretation of Cultures, pp. 87–125. New York: Basic Books.

Jean Baudrillard, The Mind of Terrorism and Why They Fight with Their Death, Prepared and Translated, Bassam Hajjar, Arab Cultural Center, Beirut, First Edition, 2003.

Mark Kukis, "My Heart Became Attached, The Strange Journey of John Walker Lindh," Brassey's Inc. 2003.

M. R. Torres, J. Jord a an, and N. Horsburgh (2006) Analysis and Evolution of the Global Jihadist Movement Propaganda, Terrorism and Political Violence, 18:399–421, 2006. Taylor & Francis Group, LLC

Olivier Roy, Globalized Islam, Translated by Lara Maalouf, Dar el-Saqi, Beirut, First Edition, 2003, p.195.

The Role of religion and belief in the fight against terrorism, OSCE Conference on The role of freedom of religion and belief in a democratic society: Searching for ways to combat terrorism and extremism Baku, Azerbaijin, 10-11 October 2002

The Islamist: Why I joined radical Islam in Britain, what I saw inside and why I left by Ed Husain, Penguin, 2007, 288 pp.

The Secret of Attraction ISIS Propaganda and Recruitment. Published in 2016 by Friedrich-Ebert-Stiftung- Jordan and Iraq

The Secret of Attraction: ISIS Propaganda and Recruitment/ Mohammad Suliman Abu Rumman et al.; translated by William John Ward et al. –Amman: Friedrich-Ebert-Stiftung, 2016

Links

http://soufangroup.com/foreign-fighters-in-syria/

http://english.al-akhbar.com/print/20017

http://www.un.org/sc/committees/1267/NSQI29911E.shtml

http://smallwarsjournal.com/jrnl/art/abu-bakr-al-baghdadi-and-the-theory-and-practice-of-jihad

https://www.ctc.usma.edu/posts/isils-political-military-power-in-iraq

https://www.ctc.usma.edu/posts/the-islamic-state-in-iraq-and-the-levant-more-than-just-a-june-surprise

https://ctc.usma.edu/islamic-state-threat-2018-fifa-world-cup/

http://gees.org/articulos/understanding-terrorism-in-the-twenty-first-century

http://www.gees.org/files/article/20022010093237_Analisis-07561.pdf

https://www.coursehero.com/file/35862595/Week-2-DQ-1docx/

https://books.google.com/books?id=ZHg2DwAAQBAJ

https://ctc.usma.edu/app/uploads/2018/05/CTC-Sentinel_Vol11Iss5.pdf

https://jaiyeorie.blogspot.com/2017/10/isis-threatens-attack-on-world-cup-2018.html

https://www.dailymail.co.uk/news/article-5599165/ISIS-threatens-Vladimir-Putin-fanatics-warn-bloody-edition-World-Cup.html

https://css.ethz.ch/content/dam/ethz/special-interest/gess/cis/center-for-securities studies/resources/docs/CTC_Sentinel- Vol11Iss5.pdf

https://www.reuters.com/article/us-russia-attacks-detentions/russia-says-thwarts-planned-islamic-state-attacks-in-moscowidUSKBN1HY1XS

https://ufdc.ufl.edu/AA00066699/00117

https://www.rt.com/sport/375838-safety-2018-world-cup/

Index

U

Y

Z